T5-BQA-626

FUNERAL GAMES

And Other Poems

Funeral Games

And Other Poems

by

Vernon Scannell

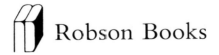 Robson Books

821
5283f

Acknowledgements are due to the editors of the following magazines in which a number of these poems first appeared: *Ambit, The American Scholar, Encounter, The Listener, The Literary Review, Poetry Australia, Poetry Review, The Spectator, Stand, Times Literary Supplement, Two Plus Two, The Yale Literary Magazine;* also to the Tate Gallery and the BBC.

First published in Great Britain in 1987 by Robson Books Ltd., Bolsover House, 5-6 Clipstone Street, London W1P 7EB.

Copyright © 1987 Vernon Scannell

British Library Cataloguing in Publication Data

Scannell, Vernon
Funeral games and other poems.
I. Title
821'.914 PR6037.C25

ISBN 0-86051-429-3 *89-3418*

Typesetting by Concept Communications (Design & Print) Ltd
Printed in Great Britain by
St Edmundsbury Press Ltd, Bury St Edmunds, Suffolk
Bound by Dorstel Press Ltd, Harlow, Essex

Contents

IN MEMORIAM P.A.L., 2.12.85   7

FUNERAL GAMES   9

CANDLE REFLECTIONS   10

APPLE POEM   12

THE LAST KING   14

THE LONG AND LOVELY SUMMERS   16

WHEN THE BOUGH BREAKS   18

THE HOUSE   20

WHITE WITCH   22

THE LONG FLIGHT   24

IN GOLDEN ACRE PARK, LEEDS   26

BICYCLE RACES, ROUNDHAY PARK, LEEDS   27

A VICTORIAN HONEYMOON   28

HANDS   30

A DISTANT PROSPECT (CLASS PHOTOGRAPH, 1930)   32

SIXTY-FIRST BIRTHDAY POEM   34

OLD MAN   35

OLD MAID   36

GRANDFATHER'S TEARS   37

GRANDMA IN WINTER   38

BONA DEA   39

COMPANY OF WOMEN   40

AUTUMNAL   45

NEIGHBOURS   46

SEPARATE ROOMS   47

GREAT WESTERN RAILWAY TERMINUS, 1938   48

HEADLINES   49

FILM SHOOTING   50

DRINKING UP TIME   52

FIGHTING TALK   53

SKIRTS AND TROUSERS   54

NAMING OF POETS   56

COLLECTED POEMS RECOLLECTED   58

SENTENCES   60

In Memoriam P.A.L., 2.12.85

I heard the news at one o'clock,
Formal from the radio;
The room seemed sharply cold as though
The air itself had suffered shock.

I was surprised by how those words,
So calmly voiced, could penetrate
The idling heart and resonate
Like softly falling minor thirds.

We met each other once, that's all,
Nearly twenty years ago.
We were not close and yet I know
His death-day stretched beneath a pall

Of melancholy that would leave
Something of its gloom behind,
A broken cord, half-lowered blind,
Although we may forget we grieve.

Of all that happened on that day
Of snivelling December rain
One thing chiefly chimes again:
I did not weep or curse or pray,

But petulantly cried aloud,
'I do not want him to be dead!'
He would have smiled to hear this said,
If he had heard from some high cloud.

Yet I believe that smile would be,
Although ironic, kindly too,
For who would approbate the true
Voice of feeling more than he?

Funeral Games

The slow, black bell seems still to nod, its shadow
Trembles in the gloom, a musky perfume
Faint in the ear and mingling with the sweet
Blue smoky exequies and far receding chop
Of plodding hooves as she again goes in
Through their familiar door and moves inside
The still shocked house. She visits each dazed room
Leaving till last his favourite one – his books,
So many, everywhere, as if, progenitive,
They multiplied and spilled from shelves and chairs;
The recorded Brandenburgs, the piano-lid
Still raised and on the music-rest the Liszt
Consolation Number Three, the pages cold,
And, underneath the window, on his desk
Pencils and speechless sheets of lined A4
With one apart on which a few words walk,
A poem, perhaps, a letter to the times;
It does not matter now. She hoped to touch
And be consoled by something of him here
But nothing can dissolve or penetrate
The robe of ice her heart elects to wear;
These things, his toys, important trivialities,
The best of him maybe, but only toys,
As he and she might be the artefacts
And toys of hands from which they have been dropped,
Once greatly loved and cared for, but not now,
Left in different rooms to feed on dust.

Candle Reflections

i

A yellow whisper in the still midnight,
A single syllable, inverted heart,
Bright petal glimmering behind dark glass,
Its thick white stem unseen by the watcher
Who stands beneath the elm in the lane,
His eyes eager for the arranged message
Of warning or promise: 'Go. Keep away.
He is here!' or 'Come now, oh my love. Yes. Come!'

ii

On a summer morning a periwigged forebear
Would see on his desk in the sun's brightness
Among litter of manuscripts, pens and pipes
His nocturnal helpmeet, now exhausted,
Sunk to its chest in its melted swoon,
Squat in its holder, small glazed ruff,
The night's work done. Now in dark cupboards
And dusty drawers they repose like dead brides.

iii

Remembered marriage of honey and wax,
Conjunction of sweetness and light, gold halo-ing
The child's fair head at sleeping time,

White presences on silver occasions,
Star-flowering in bell's breath on snowy pasture,
Celebrations at commemorative festivals,
Their tears silent, warm and lenitive,
Cooling to translucent blebs, like pearls.

iv

Their element has always been religious. They
Proliferate in cathedrals, scenting the gloom;
They pray, in chapels, prayers of extreme
Simplicity; their aspect delights children,
It consoles the old; they invigilate
The explanations of the dead, stand sentinel
About the draped catafalque. When power fails
And all the lights go out, they will be needed.

Apple Poem

Take the apple from the bowl or bough
Or kitchen table where in gloom it glows
And you will sense, mysteriously, how
Its fragrant and substantial presence throws
A shadow shape of this one's red and green,
Whatever it may be – Rose of Bern,
Spice Pippin, Golden Russet, Hawthorn Dean –
Across the mind and then you may discern
Through every sense the quintessential fruit,
Perfected properties all apples own,
In this platonic shadow; absolute
This pleasing thing that you alone have grown.

Beneath the apple's skin, its green or gold,
Yellow, red or streaked with varied tints,
The white flesh tempts, sharp or sweet, quite cold.
Its blood is colourless; scent teases, hints
At othernesses that you can't define;
The taste of innocence, so slow to fade,
Persists like memory. This fruit is wine
And bread; is eucharistic. It has played
Its role in epics, fairy-tales, among
Most races of the earth; made prophecies
Of marriages and kept the Norse Gods young;
Shone like moons on Hesperidian trees.

And here, domestic, familiar as a pet,
Plump as your granny's cheek, prepared to be
Translated into jam or jelly, yet
It still retains a curious mystery.

Forget the holy leaves, the pagan lore,
And that you munch on legends when you eat,
But see, as you crunch closer to the core,
Those little pips, diminutive and neat
Containers aping tiny beetles or
Microscopic purses, little beads,
Each holding in its patient dark a store
Of apples, flowering orchards, countless seeds.

The Last King

When the last King has gone into the dark
There will be mourning, though the mourners may
Not know their grieving's cause, nor even mark
That what they do is grieve. And on that day
The sun will seem unwilling to appear,
Its breathings fan unseasonably chill;
But there will be no sweating mob to cheer
The farewell speech and axeman's glinting skill
Or panic at a sudden muzzle-flash
And crack. The last King will not leave us thus.
His dying, silent, soft as falling ash,
Occurring with no ceremonial fuss,
Will be enacted in a hotel room
After his undramatic abdication,
Hearing the whisper, in the deepening gloom,
Of alien seas; his slow assassination
Performed by his own treasonous appetites.
So he will lie, the table at his side
Bearing no royal relics; the fitful lights
From curtain chink and passing cars outside
Show only his dark spectacles instead
As he, fat bag containing cooling bones
Lies incognito on the common bed.
And afterwards, no orchestra of moans,
No formal, public panoply of grief,
Gun-carriage, sleek black plume or muffled drum,
Yet his uncommon spectre, this last leaf
Now fallen from the doomed tree will become
A drifting presence, insubstantial, faint,
Ubiquitous, a whiff of something rare,

The scent of gold; heard too – complaint
Of ancient instruments on evening air –
And seen at fading moments in the night,
Gold gleam in black recess, lost coin, a glow
Of tiny lamp, quick spark, a dying light
Whose ultimate extinction we now see –
Pretender, slave, republican or clerk –
Will disinherit all, for all will be
Mysteriously diminished by that dark.

The Long and Lovely Summers

How long and lovely were the summers then,
Each misted morning verdant milk, until
The sun blurred through, at first a pallid wen
Beneath the sky's bland skin and then, still pale,
A swollen, silvery dahlia-head, before
It burned to gold on laundered gentian blue.

At noon the picnic by the waterfall,
The bright behaviour of the butterflies
Interpreting the light; the plover's call
Above the rhyming flowers, the sun-baked pies
Of cow-pats, fossilized, antique; the cool
Shades of chestnuts, little pools of night.

Night: frosted mathematics of the stars;
Homages of fragrances; the moon,
Curved kukri-blade of ice; the green guitars
And soft soprano breeze conspired to croon
Late lullabies that soothed us into dream
And on to dawn which new delights would spice.

Things are different now. The seasons mock
What expectations we may entertain.
No, things are not like that – and, taking stock,
It seems they never were. Did not grey rain
Stop play? Storms follow drought? A child was drowned.
In close-up, river nymphs were coarse and fat.

And yet we still remember them – the long
And lovely summers, never smeared or chilled –
Like poems, by heart, like poems, never wrong;
The idyll is intact, its truth distilled
From maculate fact, preserved as by the sharp
And merciful mendacities of art.

When The Bough Breaks

That the daytime's playful breeze could grow to this
Was something that could chill the heart and rip
The breath out of your chest, as the great gale could;
Something that appalled, something with such weight
To put you on your knees, compelling prayer
And trembling gestures of propitiation.
You might look at your child, that tiny rage,
And ask what incubation could start there.

The night was swollen by its bulk and brawn,
Blind giant, flailing ignorant and mad.
Our windows winced and flinched. Outside, the trees
Lashed back and wrestled at each fresh attack;
Clawed grasses shrieked, the mountains deliquesced;
Their falling waters vaporized, swept down,
Went burling through the vales, black avalanche
Of air: a murderous metamorphosis.

But in the morning's glitter all lay calm.
The mountains had climbed back into themselves.
A sly and disavowing breeze blew cool,
And counted leaves and petals where they fell.
We drove back to the city through the lanes
Where sheepish fields were smeared and blurred with cream
Of white and yellow flowers. The sky was cleansed.
Through glass it seemed that summer had returned.

Closer to the city all was changed;
Those orderly spruce avenues transformed:
On pavements twisted branches writhed and sprawled,
Their fluttering rags, weak signals of distress.
The small green armaments of conker-shells,
Whose fruit – snug, glossy jewels – would never now
Grow plump in satin darkness, had been torn
Too soon from bludgeoned chestnuts, crushed on stone.

Sun filtered through, but not with certainty.
Air hunched and shuddered every now and then,
As if remembering. Yet, just three days
Ago, we swam in silken waters, drowsed
In honey sun and listened to the low
Susurrus and soft labials of summer.
That things can change like this is something we
Should not forget, although we always do.

The House

Seen only once but unmistakable
That wink of sentience in stone and glass,
The way it seemed almost to smile. Perhaps
That sounds like anthropomorphic gush and yet
Some houses do seem able to express
Primary emotions, even make
Statements of a very simple kind.

This house that you have long been searching for
Might be discovered almost anywhere,
In some suburban road of similars,
Yet you would recognize it instantly,
As love's investigating eyes pick out
One special face among those little masks
Swirling like leaves toward the playground gate.

If isolated, out of town, the house
Would not be found where frozen mountains gash
The sky's dark temples, troubled torrents brawl
And air is curdled with acerbic cries
Of curlews' maledictions and the wind
Whines and blares its hostile messages
Round chimney-stack and rages at the panes.

It would be set where hills are vigilant,
Green charities with aprons stitched with flowers,
Rivulets make jokes among white stones;
The autumn garden would be dazed in mist,
Long grasses palming russets as they fall;
On outer walls the ivy would hold close
Its dusty secrets in the pungent dark.

The house is not impracticably large
But there are rooms and corners to surprise,
Unexpected narrow flights of stairs
And thoughtful attics where, from skylight glass,
Blue chutes of gold-dust lean towards the floor,
And from a downstairs room, just audible,
A piano floats a soft adagio.

In town or out, when winter nights come down,
The curtained windows glow, each luminous square
A box of sensual delights from which
You hear rich skeins of sound complected by
A hidden treasury of instruments.
Images of childhood Christmas there
Glitter in warm frost before they blur.

You will at last come to an open gate
Which beckons you to enter, move towards
The possible fulfilment of a wish
Born long ago, its substance now mislaid.
The path is devious and long. Dusk falls.
The trees are whispering caves. God only knows
What house, if any, waits to welcome you.

White Witch

In the village pub the men converse;
Their talk retains the slow and wondering pace
Of older, fading days. One lifts his glass
And holds it to the lamplight like a nurse
Consulting a thermometer, and then,
Reassured, he drinks, then sighs and, satisfied,
He listens, nodding, to the other men.
They speak of *her*, and keep their voices low
As if she might be listening, although
They know she must be far away inside
Her house or, farther still, locked in her dark
And unimaginable fantasies.
She drinks, they say, *gets drunk and yells and cries*
And cusses like a man or worse. She's stark
Crazy when she gets like that. Not right
It isn't, not in a woman, and a lady, too.
She must have been a beauty years ago.
Some shake their heads; the young ones mutter, grin
But furtively, as if she might look in
And see them, listen to their talk. The sight
Of her at window or on threshold would
Gorgonize each drinker where he stood.
She threatens them in ways they can't define,
So they traduce her, ridicule, although
When meeting her on her infrequent strolls
Along the village street they never fail
To greet her with a shifty deference,
Unctuous and excessively polite,
Acknowledged sometimes, though more often not.
On certain days and sometimes in the night

They hear the noises from the tall white house
Beyond the church, the sound of smashing glass
And then those jagged and forsaken howls,
Until the stealthy ambulance arrives
With bandages of silence and soft dark.
When she has gone they feel her presence still
And see her image, white and terrible,
A haunted ruin; yet wisps of splendour stay,
Frail ghosts of glory. a house once beautiful
Now fallen into moribund decay,
And they, the villagers, are like their own
Neat cottages and bungalows which, seen
From Beacon Hill – a distant view – are small
As children gathered round the summer green,
And safe, because they have not far to fall.

The Long Flight

*. . . a German Dornier bomber crashed
into a ploughed field in North Wales
and lay undetected for 43 years. The
plane, with its bomb load intact, was
shot down on its way to Liverpool on
October 16, 1940 and buried itself in
the soft ground, killing all the crew.*

The Guardian 28.9.83

From darkening Cherbourg airfield they took off
At twenty hundred hours, young crews but tough
And hardened to their work, a bomber squadron
Of Dornier Seventeens. They headed on
Towards the English Channel, their target Liverpool.
Hard to spot against the smeared autumnal
Skies they looked, from earth, like iron crosses
Or, black against pale lunar breast, like brooches,
Bird-shaped, sliding into folds of dark.
And soon, above the Wessex coast, the crack
And thud of anti-aircraft guns hurled up
Their brilliancies of rage, the probe and dip
Of searchlights swung like white sticks of the blind.
One plane was hit. It lurched and bucked, then climbed
But fiery pennants flew from starboard wing
Until the wind's rush ripped them off and flung
Them down to the floor of night. The plane went on
Though engine-cough said damage had been done
And slowly altitude and speed decreased
Till they had lost all contact with the rest.
And so, alone, the broken aircraft droned
Low over Denbigh Moor then turned for home.

Too late. Its single engine faltered, cut:
The pilot snarled and sweated as he fought
To bring back power. The crew was clenched and white,
Silent as the drowned. The plane's nose dipped
And through the wind's black howl they plummeted
To where ploughed earth was goffered like the sea
And, like the sea, earth hungered for the crew.
The plane went down; it sank in troughs of soil,
Down into darkness, deep in loam and marl,
Silent, dark as ocean's shifting gloom.
Then spectral engines purred again: they flew,
Flew blind with shattered instruments for more
Than forty years in fossil silence, war,
With never hope of armistice. Now gulls
And curlews wheel and cry above, their calls
Bleak requiem for what they see down there –
The shadowed shape, the giant bird entombed,
Wings cruciform as if it rode the air.

In Golden Acre Park, Leeds

The sunlight is fresh poured, liquescent gold,
Transparent, yet its body can be felt.
The roses and the rhododendrons float
In verdancy of leaves and fern and yield
Their innocent convictions to the wide
And cloudless stare of blue. And, over there
Past shimmering skin of pond, past beech and fir,
Keeping to the careful paths, the staid
And well-pressed man of later middle-age,
Clean-shaven, solid, shiny-booted, walks
And does not see or hear dark starry larks
And boisterous blackbirds musically enlarge
Upon this jewelled morning in July.
His step is blind, mechanical; his eyes
Are glacial, fixed ahead as if he sees
A frozen bleak horizon far away
From this rejected luxury of air
And colour. Tucked with care beneath one arm,
Packed neatly, like a family snapshot album,
His prudent waterproof is held secure,
A tidy parcelling of navy-blue
Containing rain-seeds, memories of war,
Dark clouds, a little thunderbolt or two.

Bicycle Races, Roundhay Park, Leeds

From far above the amphitheatre's green,
Shrunken by distance, each rider and machine
Are fused into a single thing, alive,
Insectile. Arched backs and beetle heads contrive,
With spindle limbs, to move on shimmering rings
Of fine-spun webs; the starter's pistol stings
Silence like a Christmas-cracker's snap
As they surge forward for the opening lap.
When we draw closer to the track we can
Dissect each insect into thing and man,
And, nearer yet, proximity reveals
The frantic knees, like twiddling thumbs, the wheels
Sizzling on the labile grass below
The ram's-horn handlebars, the wheels that show
How spokes of ice have melted in hot speed,
A silvery blur. The winner's head, black bead,
Is lifted, as he rides across the line,
And, humanized, he smiles. The circled shine
Of spokes now flickers, ticking down, each wheel
Seen first as fine-sliced lemon, then as steel
And rubber now the spell of speed has fled.
The other riders finish, every head
Stays down, seems bowed in misery or shame.
Every man is numbered, but his name
Will be restored when evening comes and he
Puts on his clothes of full humanity,
Drives home, his bicycle strapped on the roof
Of car or van, upturned, a trophy, proof
Of having hunted with the brave; and so
Its wheels, revolving slowly in the flow
Of darkening breeze, may faintly rhyme with how
Shot prey's dead limbs might stir; these wheels could swing
The pendant heart, like some once living thing.

A Victorian Honeymoon

Her features in the frame are pale and blurred
Imprisoned in the glass. Her hairbrush soars
And swoops and rises like an ivory bird
About her stormy head. The misty gauze
Of chiffon at her breast is startled by
A rose's crimson wound; her gaze implores
Reprieve, or answer to her brimming 'Why?'

And there is no reply. She knows that she
Must grow accustomed to this bitter taste,
The gravy of despair. Outside, the sea
Repeats incessant prophecies of waste
And now its slow, unvaried voice contains
A salt intelligence which must be faced:
There is no hope of rescue from these chains.

The links are insubstantial, and they seemed
Not long ago to gleam, a golden prize,
The goal of which, since girlhood, she had dreamed,
Its aureate sparkle dancing in her eyes;
But now, they are custodial; these chains
Are fetters on the spirit; they chastise
Insulted flesh with unimagined pains.

It was another world when it, and she –
Or, rather, that seraphic girl who died,
Whose days were like a charmed eternity
Of summer picnics – were transmogrified:
Green paradise transformed to tenebrous cave.
Her beauty torn, voice shrilled. The tales had lied:
No hope of princely rescue by the brave.

Her husband soon will come and she must smile;
She cannot tell him that it hurts. All day
They trudged the foreign pavements, mile on mile –
Museums, churches, statues – then the bay
As sunset bled across the sky and sea;
Sad twilight as the pilgrimage of grey
And hooded waves moved shoreward endlessly.

Then back to this. She smells tobacco-smoke.
It sickens her. She thinks she hears his tread
Outside the door. She feels self-pity choke,
A bitter caustic potion: pain and dread
Compose their plaint, but pride aborts the cry;
It freezes in the glass; she lifts her head
And sees reflected eyes, resigned and dry.

Hands

Hands can be eloquent, though sometimes they
Mislead us utterly in what they say.
I have seen slender-fingered, candle-white
Supple and fluent hands that many might
Call 'sensitive', 'a pianist's hands', 'artistic';
But these were owned by someone mean, sadistic,
Hostile to art, a gross materialist.
I know another man, fine pianist,
Whose powerful, sausage-fingered, meaty fists
Should hang from goal-keeper's or butcher's wrists,
Yet on the gleaming keys these hands could wake
Ghosts of drowned nightingales in starry lakes.
I knew a fighter, too, fast welterweight,
Whose punches could crack bone and could create
Sudden shattered galaxies in the head,
Yet from his hands alone you might have said
That he was not unusually strong,
For they were hairless, pale, the fingers long.
So many hands will tell us lies, but I
Have never known old labouring men's deny
Their simple character: these never lie.
For years they have manhandled spade or hook,
Shovel, axe or pick until they look
Like weathered tools, mattock, hammer, vice,
Battered, annealed by wind and sun and ice.
I like to watch them rest on tables, knees,
Lifting a pint of beer or with deft ease
Rolling a fag which later burns between
Dark oaken knuckles which have never been
Surely as soft and sensitive to pain

As this pen-pusher's hand I look at now;
But most of all I like to witness how
They lift small, tired grandchildren and hold
Them curled and safe, how gently they enfold
Their always welcome, always cherished guests,
Become protecting, gnarled and living nests.

A Distant Prospect
(Class photograph, 1930)

This was Standard Three, the school Church Street
Junior Boys', Beeston, Nottinghamshire.
You can tell that it was summer by the way
The children squint and wrinkle at the gaze
Of prophecy as lens and pupil meet.

Also the way they're dressed is a thermometer:
Shirts or jerseys, though a few have come
In Sunday jackets, unaccustomed ties.
This small élite has, pinned on its lapels,
Badges of office, each boy a monitor.

These frown responsibly. And you can tell
By strictly parted hair, its recent wet
Submission to the comb or brush, that they
Might one day be full corporals, shop-stewards,
Under-managers. They will do quite well,

Though few or none will ever own commissions,
Desks or telephones. The unpromoted,
Their heads close-cropped or rough as coconuts,
Grin or scowl. Here and there you see
A stare of undeceivable suspicion.

Three of the boys are specky-four-eyes. Their
Wearing glasses does not imply a legendary
Love of learning: bad eyesight, that is all.
You look at these small faces and you smell
Their element, the grey imprisoned air.

Is one of them the nine-year-old you were?
It's possible. You only know that now
Those few suspicious sceptics seem to see
A menace in the black-cowled camera,
Cold glitter in the lens's inky glare.

Sixty-first Birthday Poem

This is the age at which the bodies
Of unidentified men are found
In streets near public houses or
On tow-paths or waste-ground,
Foul play never suspected; an inch or less
In the middle pages of the local press.

It is the age at which young women
Do not, in fact, avert their gaze;
If their brilliant eyes should chance upon you
They wipe you out like death-rays.
That you might still claim a little virility
Does not reduce your invisibility.

It is the age when all ambition
Has fossilized, each aspiration
Replaced by muted desperation
Or muffling fog of resignation;
No candles for your cake today;
No cake for candles anyway.

The only card in the morning's post
Is from the Department of Disease
And Total Insecurity.
No birthday gifts; there'll be no knees-
Up later at the Horse and Groom:
Today you've got the key of the tomb.

And yet you grin and tap your toe
To the tune of a silent song today,
And it must be lively by the look of you;
'Senile dementia,' is what they would say,
Those men in white coats. But, no matter what,
Hang on to it, pal: it's all that you've got.

Old Man

What he wished to be and what he was
No longer brawl; the grunts and thuds are dumb.
A former bandit in a fat disguise,
No longer prone to injure anyone,
Holster empty and his tired eyes red,
He nods in ancient rocking chair and sighs,
Remembering that lovely loaded gun,
But then recalls the various salt he shed,
And what a nuisance it so often was.
'Great days, all gone; dear comrades, all stone dead.'
He loves them, for the dead do not condemn
Or mock or boss, or say he's telling lies,
But smile and whisper from the darkening gloom,
'You're tired and cold. Come in. It's time for bed.'

Old Maid

Pallor is her one distinctive feature.
Her hair and eyes are pale; her meagre lips
Profess no natural or artful colour.
Resigned to taking tea in milky sips,
Entirely feminine, yet less than woman,
At forty-five she uses words that chink
Like pence in red tin money-boxes: Heaven
Is where her Daddy is. She does not drink.

Lover of cats and curates she endorses
Slack platitudes, convention's thoughtless sketch,
Has walked on in a score of sniggering farces,
Been chained in chapters as a witch or wretch.
Yet she endures the darkly understood
Raw and chronic wound of womanhood.

Grandfather's Tears

He cries easily now who once maintained
That weeping was a woman's recreation,
His sedentary grief, lubricious tears,
Induced by simulacra of real pain,
Parodies of pathos on the screen –
The blue-eyed death of child or faithful dog,
Honest cop or genial soda-jerk –
Pacific interludes between the bouts
Of stabbing, shooting, putting in the boot.
There are even times when throat and eyes
Flood with compassion at the sight of ads
For dog-food, baby-powder or shampoo,
But never when the unembellished truth
Of newsreels is presented, images
Of famine, torture, violence in the streets.
Grandpa is bored. He goes out for a pee
Or shuffles up to bed.
                          Old man, old baby,
Off you go. Sleep well. You've had your fill
And more of actuality: two wars,
Insult, hunger, treachery and shame,
The ceaseless accusation from the fields
Of darkness and white stones, the whispering
From buried legions of the faceless dead.
Have your good cry which does not hurt at all;
Enjoy that warm release and go to bed.

Grandma in Winter

In her black shawl she moves over the field of snow
With a slow proud strut, like a burgher
Or a fat crow.
The raw sun has oozed on to the lint of cloud,
A pretty smear of pain. The church gathers its little ones,
The stone children, about its skirts
And tells them an old story.

She will join them, stand perfectly still and quiet there.
No-one will notice her.
And when night unfolds
Its old black umbrella with the little holes
She will pray for the blond stones and the friable bones,
The blue melted jellies; those white
Teeth, the small blanched almonds.

Bona Dea

Who can this someone be, this lady walking
Under the frown of yews and cypresses,
Pouting her great pale belly? You have seen her before.
She is, and will be again, someone's mother:
The beak and plumage look familiar.

Here belly is hard-boiled, a white chamber-pot;
She is Señora Humpty-Dumpty below the breast.
Do not chance another keek down there though
As she moves slowly past on her smooth castors.
Her fingers are pale snakes.

Supper-time. She perches on a stone chair
And scoops spaghetti from a bowl of bone.
The sauce is a mix of incantation and theology,
It smells of sins and psalms.
She is eating for two.

When her meal is finished she folds her napkin;
It is stained with mystery. It has wrapped up
Chewed meat and grass, excreta of phantoms,
False teeth and testimony. When the stars titter
Her long stare freezes them.

Company of Women

Miss Steeples

Miss Steeples sat close;
She touched me.
Her hands were white,
Fingernails pink
Like shells of prawns.
They tapped my desk
And, as she murmured,
Numbers blurred.
She smelled of spring
And cool cash chemists.
One summer evening,
Not by chance,
I met her walking
Near the green
Court she beautified
Dressed in white.
In one hand swung
A netted catch
Of tennis balls.
She smiled and said,
'Hello.'
She smiled.
Love-punctured
I could not answer.

At the end of the summer
She went away.
It was her smell I loved
And her fingernails

ii

Thelma

Thelma was a Brownie.
I never spoke to her
Although we spent a year together
In Standard Three.
I once followed her home
From the Brownie HQ.
There was honeysuckle in the gardens;
Songs of gramophones, too.
The satchel she brought to school
Was made of expensive leather
And in her hair
She wore a slide of tortoiseshell,
My first fetish.
We never spoke,
Not once in all that time.
It was a long spell
And is not over:
When I smell honeysuckle now
It is Thelma I smell.

iii

Doris

Doris was fifteen.
Under her unsuitable blouse
Her breasts bounced when she ran.
I kissed her once
And she fled
Giggling and joggling home.
MacFeeney cheered like a football crowd.
I made his nose bleed.
Doris was more exciting
Than cigarettes,
Sweeter than caramels,
More sparkling than sherbert.
For thirteen weeks I saved
To buy her a gift:
It looked like a sucked pear-drop
On a thin chain.
I like to think of it, snug
Between those plump bubs,
Those joys
That age has never withered.
MacFeeney keeps a pub in Mablethorpe.

iv

Kathleen

Kathleen was tall.
My eyes grew dizzy when they climbed
Her legs;
Sometimes they fell.
Her hair was rich
And golden red,
It glowed like fire
Reflected in
Good marmalade.
We walked at night
Under a nervous sky,
Its darkness probed and drenched
By searchlights, jets
Of phosphorescent milk
Thrilling the black air.
Marauding engines grumbled
As we played
With high explosives
Of primed limbs and lips;
Incendiary kisses fell.
My hands grew dizzy when they climbed
Her legs
But did not fall.
At her long cry
All sirens held their tongues,

Her hair was drenched, it spread
Wild and impenitent,
A red and morning cloud
Above a wasted town
That smouldered but already stirred,
Would rise up new again.

v

Barbara

Barbara was small
But in that little space
A charge of sexual voltage hummed
And, when released, it singed and dazzled mad.
I gave her poetry to read:
She judged it 'very nice',
Would rather far
Been offered chocolate or kisses.
One winter night, the pubs all shut,
She crouched beneath the frosty stars
And pissed.
She looked up, grinning, as the glitter hissed.
And that is what I most remember,
Less passion than delight,
More mischief than dark moans –
Quick sparkle, hiss and rising mist,
The frosty stars
And Barbara twinkling wantonly
And wild.

Autumnal

He walks slowly along Cathedral Road and hears
Funereal music in the misty dark.
Leaves tapestry the pavement, days of rain
Have blurred that veined precision, silencing
The drily whispered commentary again.
Beneath a bilious lamp pulped yellows, browns
And slippery blacks are mushed, all definition
Lost as his slow, browsing shoes move through
The mawkish narrative of mortal summer,
Doomed passion poisoned by the murderous hours
And picked by needle minutes to the bone.
Arriving at a house of blinded words
He pauses, enters, climbs up to the room
Where empty bottles, echoes of the dead
Who fell in ancient, half-forgotten battles
Rehearse the perfect silence of a tomb.
The music freezes in his wounded head.

Neighbours

She:
'Leave, my love, before the morning
Drains the darkness from the pane.
Others who ignored this warning
Did not live to love again.

'Stars, those frozen birdsong fragments,
Soon will melt and disappear;
Footsteps on the frosty pavements
Tap out signals you should fear.'

He:
'How, my dearest, can I hasten
From your clinging limbs and lips
Now warm folds of blind sensation
Cause a rational eclipse?

'What if curtain-peeping neighbours
Recognize the man they see?
Let them wave their stage-prop sabres,
They can't injure you and me.'

She:
'Ah, my love, I fear night's ending
Not because your dawn-lit face
Would feed the need of those intending
Our exposure and disgrace.

'What I dread is our own gazing,
In the light that tells no lies,
At each other, neighbours, facing
Features we don't recognize.'

Separate Rooms

She lies and smiles in sleep
Ten Tarquin strides away,
Still tastes his nightcap kiss;
Her goodnight whisper stays,
Cavatina in the dark
Auditorium of the heart.
He settles round his grin –
Love's voluntary gull –
Sucks juice from rind of moon,
Supernal, lustral gin;
Picks golden straws from hair
And stores them with her words
In velvet secrecy,
As if quite unaware
These trinkets, which he hoards,
Are pretty trash, and when
Grey day comes barging in
Their glitter will be dimmed;
And, if her sleeping smile
Was caused by dreams of some
Other man than him,
He will not feel much pain
Till night calls up the moon
And in that room again –
Now miles away from this –
She lies and smiles, awake,
And tastes another's kiss.

Great Western Railway Terminus, 1938

The night is sad with rain and sighed farewells;
In each lamp's nimbus needles spin and flicker.
The shelter eaves are strung with nervous bells
Which fall, unchiming, bursting in quick silver.

Two lovers sit like one two-headed creature,
Locked on the platform seat, keyed with desire,
Hiding their little flame from windy weather
And all that wants to slaughter such frail fire.

The waiting locomotive snorts and huffs;
A hissing cloud of steam, a weightless dumpling,
Conceals the kissing lovers with grey fluff;
A whistle starts its chill and painful probing.

The slam of doors. One lurch, the platform settles.
The steam-cloud fades and drifts away, then shows
Again the seat, where no warm lovers nestle:
But two cold strangers, staring at their toes.

Headlines

Doctor's victim photographed in the nude;
Outbreak of foot-and-mouth spreads in South-West;
Father of five murdered in family feud;
Peace demonstrators gaoled; Miners protest;
Religious fanatic murders teacher and eats her;
Headless jogger found; All feared lost
In desert crash; Vicar strips schoolgirl and beats her.

Turn to the Personal Ads: *Grateful thanks*
To St Jude from Mike; Bunny – please phone – love Brown Eyes;
More words from the lonely, the loveless, con-men and cranks,
So try the Sports Section: *Mexican boxer dies;*
Soccer violence – three youths killed. Not worth
A glance at the Overseas page: nothing is there
But carnage by war or disease. The face of the earth
Is battered and gashed and bleeding, the face of despair,
The face of the dead Mexican fighter, all the appalled
And appalling masks of the murdered, the stares behind bars.
Scrunch up the paper, thrust away the mauled
And broken images, the festering scars.

They will burn well. The peaceful pages, too,
Will blaze and be devoured in morning's grate;
The flagrant lies and what could just be true,
The chronicles of lust and love and hate,
Rage and madness, even hope; the names,
Obscure, renowned, of slave and potentate,
All will be swallowed by impartial flames
Tomorrow – or some not so distant date.

Film Shooting

See how they fall, how many ways there are:
Operatic in their own embrace,
Back-flipping over table-top or bar
With gargling yell, disintegrating face,
Arms conducting great finales, or,
Like joke mendacious anglers, wide apart,
Or clutching belly with both hands before
Making deep obeisance as they start
The slow collapsing journey to the floor.

Their costumes alter with the changing scene:
In desert, prairie, on the dusty track
That snakes through scrub towards the dark ravine
They wear the Western villain's garments – black
And battered stetson, shirt and neckerchief.
They need a shave. On modern battlefield,
In Europe or the East, they come to grief
In khaki, grey or green, the face concealed
By helmet-shade and camouflaging leaf.

The urban victims' dress may vary more,
But snappy suits and tipped fedoras are
The usual gear; they croak in liquor store,
In sidewalk filth or, like a blackened star,
Might power-dive from the sky. They could, instead,
Be drilled in restaurant or while at stool,
In some broad's swell apartment on the bed,
Outside a movie-house or by the pool;
There's plenty of locales for getting dead.

Whenever shooting happens we see red
Expressed from neat-punched wound, a signet set
In flesh, soft sealing-wax that runs. The head
Stays more or less intact. That pirouette
Is fake, rehearsed; take it from one who knows.
I was myself once shot though thank the Lord
Not fatally, as you might well suppose
Could camera objectively record
My cadaverous appearance in repose.

Drinking up Time

Thin trill of bell, a quick bright jet which sounds
Again, sharp auditory chill in smoke
And heated cachinnation of the bar.
The clock's black sleight of hands again astounds –
Last orders called; supplied. Damp towels cloak
Pump-handles, like caged parrots, for the dark.

On the table-top geometry of rings
Is wiped away. We grip the last half-inch
With shifty grins. The end has now begun.
There's no reprieve. The yawning doorway brings
Rumours of the night; we blink and flinch,
Drinking up time, as we have always done.

Fighting Talk

I overhear the woman in the bar:
'They fought like cat and dog,' she says, her lips
Clamped tight and sour, an operation scar.
Her friend nods glazed agreement as she sips
Another gin and tonic. Both are wrong,
For cats and dogs don't fight. When dogs attack
Most cats will run. The exceptionally strong
In spirit stand, sizzling with curved back.
And then the dog will stop and growl and glare,
Retreat within its skin, then slink away.

Human couples fight – no question there –
But not like cat and dog, nor like I'd say,
Any pair of beasts. When couples rise
To slug it out their rage does not diminish
Though they might smile. You see in those cold eyes
That this fight has no rules, is to the finish.

Skirts and Trousers

It is a fact – or would have been until
About a half a century ago –
That any picture showing Jack and Jill
Would carefully preserve the status quo
And represent the boy as wearing some
Type of trousers with his manly shirt
To clothe his legs and privy parts and bum,
While Jill of course would wear some kind of skirt.

Not quite the same today. Some women wear
Trousers all the time (I mean as fact
As well as metaphor). Most choose a pair
For work or play, some simply to attract –
On certain female shapes they look sublime –
And yet I sometimes feel, I must confess,
Regret for those lost days, that faded time
Of whispering hem, that unambiguous dress.

I've often wondered why it's always been
The woman clad in skirts, the man in breeks –
At least here, on the European scene –
Though come to think of it, the ancient Greeks
(The males I mean) wore skirts, the Romans too,
And both held to the view that those who wore
Trousers were barbaric; it's still true
Some Scots wear skirts, by which they set great store.

But in the main, I think it's true to say
That, in most countries we call civilized,
Skirts are emblematic and convey
Essential woman, always recognized,
And yet I wonder why this should be so:
Why bifurcated garments for the man
While women slide both legs inside one O.
We're led back to the place where we began.

I'd take a bet that women's clothes were all
Designed, as now, by men, to satisfy,
Ever since Mankind's primeval Fall,
The same old pride of life and lust of eye
Still catered for today: but something more
Practical: a help when taken short
In labour or providing access for
The randy hunter out for easy sport?

Perhaps. Yet there is something magical
In women wearing skirts. They may look pert
In jeans, but if you seek the lyrical,
Heart-haunting woman, she will wear a skirt;
That single sleeve, concealing in its dusk
Two limbs that glimmer, brush and cross like beams
Of light, contrives a spell, a spectral musk
Which drifts into the coverts of men's dreams.

Naming of Poets

Surprising once, splendid or absurd
The names with which their mums and dads baptized
Those baby boys. A name is more than word;
It is a kind of garment, loose, outsized,
One which the child will slowly grow to fit.
My God, it must have taken years for those
Poor nippers easily to move and sit
Relaxed in such odd vests their parents chose –
Siegfried, Rudyard, Humbert, Algernon, Bysshe.
Later kids were luckier, I suppose,
Were labelled closer to the way they'd wish.

Yet even then got stuck with names in tales
From women's magazines or nominal-rolls
Of public schools (unless they came from Wales),
Names like Stephen, Christopher, Paul and Charles.
But when the second war to end all wars
Had, figuratively, seen these down the drain
Those lucky fathers, safe on Blighty's shores,
Would nomenclate their young with names as plain
As British Restaurant meals, decent, prosaic –
Brian, Alan, Donald – note again
How disyllabic names are all trochaic.

The next lot, though, chose amputated trochees,
Monikers of one blunt syllable –
More fitting for back-woodsmen from the Rockies
Or for the darts-team chalked up in your local –
Pete and Ted, Ken and Fred – yet we

Became accustomed to them in the lists
Of new contributors, and now we see
Them in the Oxford Books of that and this
Without a flicker of surprise, although
I must confess I do, a little, miss
The way those aureate Julians used to glow.

Well, tough diminutives are out and we
Must now adjust to names which look and sound
Like former surnames – Blake and Craig and Lee –
These poets' full names could be switched around
Like those reversible coats that could provide
A quick disguise for crook or private eye.
But in the end the name is no sure guide
To excellence. The stuff we save to buy
And treasure might not bear a famous name
And, if it does, it's no more reason why
We choose it than a picture for its frame.

Collected Poems Recollected

(For Peter Porter)

Most of us have smiled to see them there
On market stalls, at jumble sales, in rows
On dainty shelves in twilit bookshops, where
Mild yet vulturine explorers nose
Wheezily through seventeenth-century prose
And cough and chumble in that studious air.

Rarely disturbed, these Poets stand in line,
Quaint wall-flowers few will ever ask to dance
And none invite to share good food and wine;
Though you or I might flick a friendly glance
Most look at them, if look they do, askance,
In ways to chill the bibliological spine.

You, Peter, I am confident, could reel
Their names off, get them smartly on parade –
John Greenleaf Whittier (his three names peal
More plangently than any poem he made);
John Drinkwater (his verse, pale lemonade,
May disintoxicate but scarcely heal).

The Manxman, T. E. Brown (his shut leaves hide
Stuffed blackbird in a cardboard garden), stout
Noble, Bulwer Lytton, side by side
With fair Felicia Hemans; close about
Stand Gawsworth (next to *Ditties of a Scout*),
Great Noyes and Newbolt, monitors to Pride.

More female poets: Dora Sigerson Shorter,
And Edith Sitwell still failing to impress –
Posterity, as critic, yields no quarter –
Dark waiting spaces, especially under 'S' –
Surely for Spender? . . . Silkin? . . . Please say 'Yes'!
But none for Martial artist, Peter Porter.

For twenty years I've felt your poems were meant
For private shelves at home and in the mind.
The awkward squad, the not quite excellent
Earn, all the same, some homage of a kind:
Who knows for sure where he will be consigned?
Those foothills prove the peaks magnificent.

Sentences

*Soldiers serving sentences in
Military Prisons and Detention
Barracks are officially referred
to and addressed as S.U.S's –
Soldiers Under Sentence.*

Who spiked the water at the wedding
    Held in the Sergeant's Mess?
We all know who the fellow was:
          Jay. . .
          E. . .
          S.U.S!

Who blew reveille in the dead man's ear,
    Made him get up and dress?
It wasn't the Company Bugler, but
          Jay. . .
          E. . .
          S.U.S!

Who fed the whole battalion
    On one man's rations? Guess!
Of course you know; it could only be
          Jay. . .
          E. . .
          S.U.S!

Who marched across the sea, his boots
    Bright and dry? Why, Yes!
The smartest man in the Regiment:

            Jay. . .
            E. . .
            S.U.S!

Who made the tempest halt, ground arms
    And stand at ease, no less?
The man who knew the word of command –
            Jay. . .
            E. . .
            S.U.S!

Who rode a donkey into town
    And cried in his distress?
We don't know why, but we know who:
            Jay. . .
            E. . .
            S U.S!

Who chased the Pay Corps scroungers from
    The place of holiness;
Bashed spuds on Sunday? Who but he,
            Jay. . .
            E . .
            S.U.S!

Who woke the colonel's daughter from
    Death's sleep to wakefulness?
Not Sawbones but the miracle lad,
            Jay. . .
            E. . .
            S.U.S!

Who ripped night's bandage from the eyes
      And healed men's sightlessness?
It wasn't the M.O's orderly but
                    Jay. . .
                    E. . .
                    S.U.S!

Who never wore a pip or stripe
      Yet still achieved success?
Who held the lowest rank of all?
                    Jay. . .
                    E. . .
                    S.U.S!

Who got beat up by Itie cops
      To force him to confess?
Who got put on a Two-five-two*?
                    Jay. . .
                    E. . .
                    S.U.S!

Who took the Redcaps' fists and boots,
      His face a bloody mess
And then got taken out to die?
                    Jay. . .
                    E. . .
                    S.U.S!

                    But

*Army Form 252: charge-sheet

Who swallowed wine and pissed out water,
Couldn't wake up when reveille was blown,
Who screwed Colonel Jairus's daughter,
Ate ten men's rations, all on his own,
Robbed the blind and beat up cripples,
Flogged his donkey right to the bone?

Johnny Evans, he was the fellow,
Ended up high against the bloodshot sky,
Johnny Evans, the barrack-room cowboy,
Arms stretched out like a P.T.I.
He, and another old Janker-wallah,
One each side of the man who cried
A loud reproach to his stone-deaf father
And promised Johnny, before he died,
A place that night in the Officer's Mess,
He, Johnny Evans, was a Soldier Under Sentence
          Jay. . .
          E . .
          S.U.S!